YOUR
HERB
GARDEN
COOKBOOK

Marjorie Carter

Sweetwater Press
Florence, Alabama

Published by Sweetwater Press
P.O. Box 1855
Florence, Alabama 35631

Produced by The Triangle Group, Ltd.
227 Park Avenue
Hoboken, NJ 07030

Design: Tony Meisel
Special thanks to Risa Gary of Mikasa, New York
Origination and printing: Cronion S.A., Barcelona

Printed in Spain

ISBN 1-884822-03-7

Contents

Introduction

Herbs! From spring to autumn we are blessed with an abundance of fresh herbs. Tangy, spicy, fragrant, sweet, they are the harbingers of good eating, and they are an excellent substitute for some of the more harmful condiments we are likely to use as flavorings, salt in particular.

Don't confuse herbs with spices. Herbs are the leaves of green plants, not the berries or roots. They are, with a very few exceptions, best if used freshly picked, just at the height of their fragrance and fullest flavors. Many supermarkets now regularly stock a reasonable supply, but since they are weeds, they are quite easy to grow in a small garden or even a window box. They need light and water, but otherwise can usually be left to themselves to grow in happy profusion.

The real value of herbs is in the flavors they impart to so many dishes, from appetizers to desserts. From a sprig of thyme in a fish chowder to the sweet scent of lemon verbena in a light biscuit, herbs bring a special magic to cooking and baking.

The aroma of a stew made with herbs is quite enticing, far more than one made without. And those herbs will impart a new and different taste to the simplest and most ordinary dishes.

Following is a collection of simple recipes that will broaden your culinary horizons and make you wonder how you ever managed without herbs.

Minestrone

1/4 pound mushrooms, sliced
3 garlic cloves, minced
2 onions, chopped
2 tablespoons oil
1 tablespoon fresh chopped basil
1 teaspoon fresh chopped oregano
2 bay leaves
pinch of thyme
1/2 teaspoon black pepper
3 cups crushed tomatoes
1/4 cup white wine
2 cups chicken broth
2 cups cooked kidney beans
1 zucchini, finely sliced
1 large green pepper
2 tablespoons chopped fresh parsley

Sauté mushrooms, garlic and onions in hot oil. Add seasonings, tomatoes, wine and chicken broth and simmer for 1 hour. Add the beans, zucchini, pepper and parsley and cook until vegetables are tender. Serves 4-6.

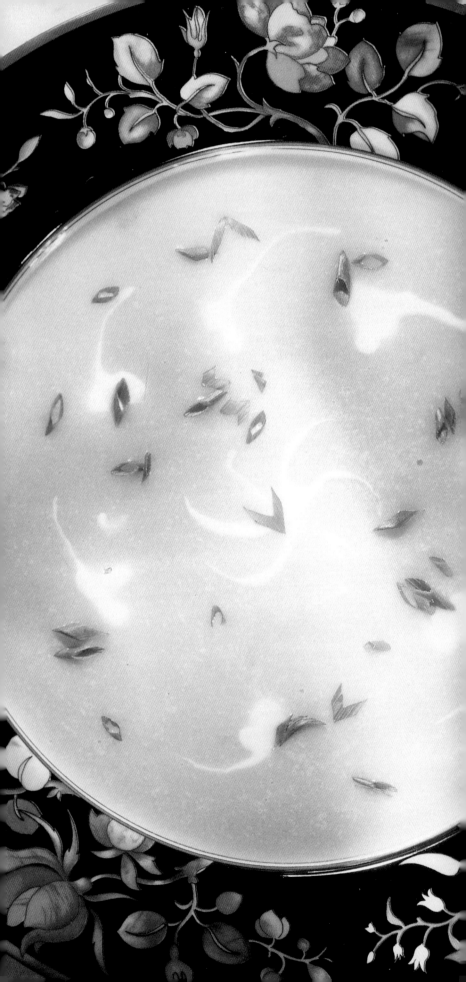

Herbed Potato Soup

6 medium potatoes, unpeeled
3 tablespoons butter
2 medium onions, chopped
1 tablespoon fresh tarragon, chopped
1/2 teaspoon white pepper
2 cups yogurt at room temperature
4 tablespoons minced chives for garnish

Steam the potatoes whole until tender. Sauté the onion
and bay in the butter. Sprinkle with the pepper. Cover and
cook over low heat for 1/2 hour. Remove skins from the
potatoes. In a blender, puree the potatoes with the onions,
removing the bay leaves first. Return to the saucepan and
whisk in the yogurt. Simmer over low heat 15 minutes,
stirring occasionally. Garnish with fresh chives. Serves 4.

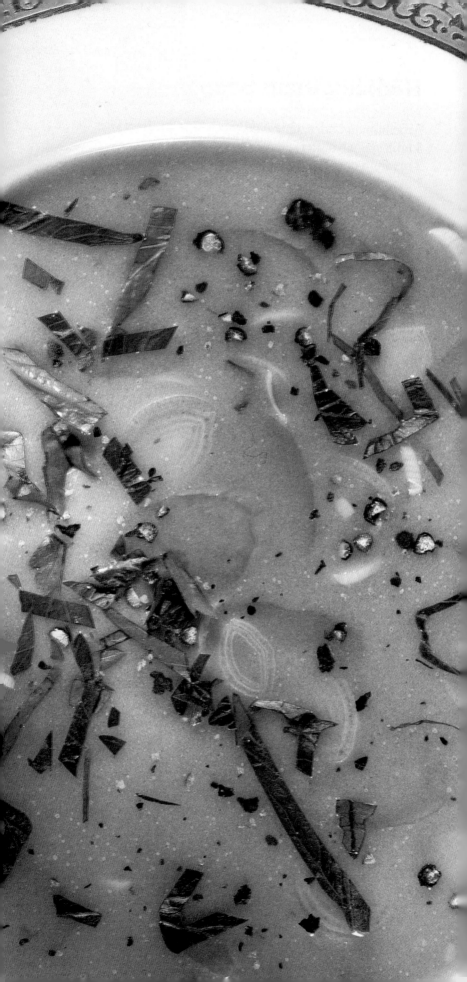

Leek Soup

2 tablespoons olive oil
4 leeks, cleaned and sliced
1 medium onion, chopped
1/4 cup celery, thinly sliced
6 cups chicken stock
2 tablespoons chopped fresh parsley
1 tablespoon chopped fresh thyme
1/8 teaspoon ground black pepper
1 pound fresh spinach, washed and drained
1/2 cup half-and-half dairy product

Sauté the leeks, onion and celery in the olive oil for 10 minutes. Place the chicken stock, sautéed vegetables, parsley, thyme and pepper in a large saucepan. Remove thick stems from the spinach and add the leaves to the stock. Bring to a boil, reduce heat and simmer 20 minutes. In blender, puree the mixture in three batches for 15 seconds each on high speed. Return to pan and stir in the half-and-half. Heat until hot, but do not boil. Serves 4-6.

Barley-Lentil Soup

2 1/4 cups raw lentils, rinsed
11 cups water
1/2 cup barley
3 bay leaves
2 cups cauliflower, chopped
2 cups broccoli, chopped
2 cups carrots, sliced
1 cup celery, sliced
1 onion, chopped
2 tablespoons fresh parsley, chopped
1 teaspoon celery seed
2 teaspoons dill weed
freshly ground black pepper
2 tablespoons vinegar

Bring lentils and water to a boil in a large soup pot. Stir in the barley and bay leaves and simmer for 1/2 hour, then add the prepared vegetables. Bring to a boil, reduce heat and simmer soup for 1 hour or until lentils are tender. Add spices and vinegar and cook for 10 more minutes. Remove the bay leaves before serving. Serves 4-6.

Stuffed Mushrooms

16 large mushrooms, cleaned
1 10-ounce package frozen spinach, chopped
1 cup low-fat cottage cheese
2 cloves garlic, minced
2 tablespoons chopped parsley
1 small onion, minced
1/2 teaspoon thyme
1/2 teaspoon dill
1/8 teaspoon nutmeg

Remove the stems from the mushrooms and chop them fine. Dip the mushroom caps in melted butter and place them on a cookie sheet. In a food processor purée the spinach, cottage cheese, garlic, onions and herbs. Combine with the chopped stems and stuff the mushrooms generously. Bake at 425 degrees F. for 12-15 minutes. Serve immediately, garnished with lemon wedges. Serves 4.

Eggplant Dip

1 medium eggplant cooked, peeled and mashed
1 tomato, peeled and chopped
1 onion, finely chopped
1 clove garlic, minced
1 tablespoon fresh oregano, chopped
1 tablespoon olive oil
1 tablespoon red wine vinegar
grated Parmesan cheese

Combine all ingredients except cheese. Spread in a shallow baking dish and sprinkle with cheese. Bake at 350 degrees F. for 15 minutes until hot and cheese is melted. Serves 4-8 as an appetizer.

Caraway Dip

8 ounces low-fat cream cheese, softened
1 cup low-fat cottage cheese
2 tablespoons caraway seed
1 tablespoon fresh chives, finely chopped
1/4 cup sherry or dry white wine
2 tablespoons milk

Cream the cream cheese with the cottage cheese. Stir in the caraway seed and the chives. Blend in the sherry or white wine and the milk. Serve with crackers or toast fingers. Serves 4-6.

Gravlad Lax

2 pounds fresh salmon fillet
1/2 cup light brown sugar
2 tablespoons coarse salt
1 bunch fresh dill

Cut the fillet into two pieces. Spread the flesh sides with
equal amounts of sugar, salt and chopped fresh dill.
Sandwich the pieces together, flesh side to flesh side in a
shallow dish. Cover with foil or plastic wrap. Place in the
refrigerator and leave for 2-4 days. Unwrap, separate the
halves and cut in very thin slices, accompanied by buttered, thinly-sliced rye bread and mustard. Serves 8
as an appetizer.

Thyme Chicken

3 pounds chicken, cut in serving-size pieces
2 tablespoons butter
1 green pepper, cut in strips
1 teaspoon dried thyme
1 teaspoon paprika
1 medium onion, sliced
1/2 cup celery, chopped
3 tomatoes, skinned and chopped
1/2 pound mushrooms, thinly sliced

Sprinkle the chicken pieces with the paprika. Melt the butter in a large skillet and brown the chicken on all sides. Add the onion, green pepper, celery, tomatoes, mushrooms and thyme. Bring to a boil and cover. Reduce the heat and simmer for 25 minutes. Serves 4.

Chicken with Garlic & Lemon Thyme

4 chicken breasts, skinned and boned
2 tablespoons extra virgin olive oil
3 large cloves garlic, crushed
2 tablespoons fresh lemon thyme, chopped
2 tablespoons fresh oregano, chopped
freshly ground black pepper
1/2 cup dry white wine

Rub the chicken breasts with the oil, garlic, herbs and pepper and set aside for 3 hours allowing the flavors to develop. Place prepared chicken in a heavy skillet, add wine and cover. Cook over low heat for 10-12 minutes, turning once, until chicken is browned outside and done in the center. Serve with rice to catch the herb juices. Serves 4.

Ground Lamb with Mint

1 1/2 pounds ground lamb
1 tablespoon oil
1/2 cup onion, finely chopped
2 tablespoons fresh parsley, chopped
3 tablespoons fresh spearmint, chopped
black pepper

Combine the lamb and the pepper, Sauté the onion in the oil. Add the onion to the lamb along with the chopped herbs. Mix well. Form into small balls and place on a baking sheet. Bake at 350 degrees F. for 25 minutes, turning once. Serve with yogurt. Serves 4.

Lamb Casserole

2 pounds lamb shoulder, cut for stew
3 tablespoons olive oil
1 pound green beans, cut in 1-inch pieces
2 large onions, sliced
1 cup chicken stock
2 tablespoons fresh dill, chopped
2 teaspoons paprika
pepper to taste

Brown meat in olive oil in casserole dish. Add remaining ingredients and season with the pepper. Cover and bake at 350 degrees F. until meat is tender, about 1 1/2 hours. Garnish with chopped mint. Serves 6.

Fusilli with Basil

1 cup chopped fresh basil leaves
1 teaspoon chopped garlic
1/2 cup pitted black olives in brine, drained and chopped
1 pound tomatoes, skinned and chopped
1/2 cup extra virgin olive oil
1 teaspoon black pepper
1 pound fusilli

Mix all ingredients but the fusilli together in a bowl and let stand for 1 hour.

Boil the fusilli in plenty of salted water until *al dente*. Drain. Toss with the uncooked sauce and serve immediately. Serves 4.

Linguine with Nasturtium Flowers

Nasturtium flowers have a sharp, peppery tang that makes them the perfect foil for oil, garlic and cheese.

1 cup shredded nasturtium flowers
2 cloves garlic, finely chopped
1 cup finely shredded arugula leaves
1/2 cup virgin olive oil
1 pound linguine
1/2 cup grated Romano cheese

Sauté the nasturtium flowers, garlic and arugula in the olive oil for 5 minutes.

Cook the linguine in boiling, salted water until *al dente*. Drain. Pour the sauce over and toss with Romano cheese. Serves 4.

Sea Scallops with Dill

3 tablespoons extra virgin olive oil
2 cloves garlic, finely chopped
1 pound sea scallops
1/2 cup dry white wine
1 tablespoon fresh dill weed, chopped

Sauté the garlic in the olive oil for 5 minutes. Add the dry scallops and cook until just heated through, about 5 minutes (if the scallops are very large, cut in half crosswise).

Add the white wine and dill and cook another 2 minutes. Serve over rice or pasta. Serves 4.

Pork Chops with Rosemary

4 large loin pork chops, closely trimmed
1/4 cup olive oil
1/2 cup lemon juice
3 cloves garlic, finely chopped
1 teaspoon crumbled rosemary
1 teaspoon black pepper

Marinate the chops in the oil, lemon juice, garlic, rosemary and black pepper for at least 1 hour.

Place the chops on a broiler rack and broil gently for about 10 minutes per side. These chops can also be cooked over charcoal. Serves 4.

Shrimp & Fresh Coriander

2 pounds large shrimp, shelled and deveined
1/2 cup lime juice
1/4 cup sesame oil
2 tablespoons chopped fresh coriander
1 teaspoon black pepper
1 small chili pepper

Marinate the shrimp in the ingredients for 2 hours.
Thread the shrimp on four skewers and grill or broil for
no more than 5 minutes, turning several times. Serves 4.

Scalloped Potatoes with Chives

2 tablespoons butter
1 tablespoon flour
1 1/2 cups milk
4 potatoes, peeled and sliced
1/2 cup sharp cheddar cheese, grated
1 tablespoon fresh chives, chopped
1 onion, chopped fine

Melt the butter and stir in the flour. Allow to cook slowly for 2 minutes. Add the warmed milk slowly, stirring constantly. Cook and stir over low heat until thickened. Add the chives. In a buttered baking dish, layer the potatoes and the onion. Pour the sauce over the top and sprinkle with grated cheese. Bake at 350 degrees F. for about 1 1/4 hours or until tender and brown and bubbly on top. Serves 4.

Glazed Onions

12 medium onions, boiled (but kept firm)
4 tablespoons butter
2 tablespoons honey
1/2 teaspoon salt
1 teaspoon fresh chervil

Arrange the boiled onions in a buttered baking dish in one layer. Melt the butter and add the honey and chervil. Cook and stir until honey is liquid. Pour over the onions to coat them. Bake at 400 degrees F. about 25 minutes. Baste the onions from time to time so they will be golden brown. Serves 4.

Honeyed Carrots

6-8 carrots, peeled and cut into 1/2-inch slices
2 tablespoons butter
1/3 cup honey
3 tablespoons fresh parsley, chopped
1 teaspoon fresh chervil, chopped
freshly ground pepper

Cook the carrots in boiling water until tender. Melt the butter and add the remaining ingredients. Heat the carrots in the sauce and serve, garnished with more fresh parsley. Serves 4.

White Bean Casserole

2 cups small white beans, soaked overnight
4 carrots, diced
1 red pepper, diced
1 stalk celery, diced
1 onion, sliced
3 garlic cloves, minced
1 bay leaf
1/2 teaspoon rosemary
1/2 teaspoon thyme
2 tablespoons olive oil
10 cups water

Drain the beans and place in a heavy soup pot with water, carrots, celery, red pepper and onion. Bring to a boil and stir in the garlic, bay leaf, rosemary, thyme and oil. Simmer over low heat for 1 hour and 45 minutes. Serves 6-8.

Minted Peas

2 pounds fresh peas, shelled
1/4 pound butter or low-fat margarine
2 tablespoons minced fresh spearmint

Cook the peas and drain. Melt the butter and add the
spearmint. Add the butter mixture to the peas and serve.
Serves 4.

Carrots with Mint

2 pounds carrots
2 tablespoons butter
1 tablespoon sugar
3 tablespoons chopped fresh mint

Quarter the carrots and steam until tender. Drain and
return to the pan. Add the butter and sugar. Stir over very
low heat for 3 minutes. Cover and cook 2 minutes more.
Add the mint and serve. Serves 6.

Zucchini with Herbs

2 pounds zucchini
4 tablespoons olive oil
2 tablespoons butter
3 cloves garlic, crushed
1 tablespoon chopped fresh chives
2 tablespoons chopped fresh tarragon
2 tablespoons chopped fresh parsley

Cut the zucchini into 1/8-inch slices. Sauté in a skillet in
hot oil for about 5 minutes. Drain the zucchini. Melt the
butter in the skillet, then add the cooked zucchini. Add
the garlic and herbs and mix well. Serve hot. Serves 6.

Fresh Basil Salad

1 head lettuce
2 tomatoes cut in round slices
1/2 pound Swiss cheese in julienne strips
1/2 cup fresh basil leaves
olive oil, to taste
basil wine vinegar, to taste
1 tablespoon mixed salad herbs (tarragon, marjoram
    and chives)
1 tablespoon lemon juice

Layer the tomato slices, Swiss cheese and basil leaves on
a bed of lettuce. Combine the olive oil, vinegar, salad
herbs, and lemon juice to taste. Shake well and pour over
the salad. Serves 4.

Tabbouleh Salad

1 cup bulgur (cracked wheat)
2 cups boiling water
2 cups parsley, finely chopped
1/2 cup scallions, chopped
1/2 cup fresh mint, chopped
1/2 cup lemon juice
1/4 cup olive oil
3 ripe tomatoes, chopped

Pour the boiling water over the wheat and let stand for 1/2 hour. Drain well and return it to the bowl. Add the parsley, scallions, mint, and lemon juice. Blend well and chill. Just before serving, toss with the oil and add the chopped tomatoes. Serves 4.

Hot Potato Salad

1 1/2 pounds new potatoes
2 tablespoons onion, finely chopped
3 tablespoons olive oil
1 tablespoon white wine or herb vinegar
2 tablespoons chopped fresh sweet marjoram

Wash the potatoes and cook them in their skins. Peel if desired, and cut into quarters. Stir in the chopped onion and the marjoram. Combine the oil and vinegar and pour over the hot potatoes. Mix gently. Serves 4-6.